The Old San Juan Walking Tour

The book for adventurous travelers who want to know it all about America's most beautiful city

Orlando Mergal, MA

©2007-2022, Orlando Mergal
Reproduction of this document, in part or in full, is prohibited.

To all those fellow travelers who like to explore the world on their own and make things up as they go...

Enjoy

Table Of Content

Introduction 1

Plaza Dársena to Paseo de La Princesa 3

Paseo de La Princesa to Plaza de la Rogativa 9

Plaza de la Rogativa to Fort San Felipe del Morro 19

Colonial Sanitarium to Plaza San José 29

Plaza San José to San Juan Museum 39

Plaza San José to El Parque de las Palomas 45

El Parque de las Palomas to Plaza Colón 53

Fort San Cristóbal 61

Fort San Cristóbal to Plaza Dársena 73

Reference Section 77

Old San Juan Walking Tour Route 80

Copyright

A Day In Old San Juan was an original work of art conceived, created and registered at the U.S. Copyright Office as a series of audio recordings in 2007. Hence, the book that you have in your hand today "The Old San Juan Walking Tour" can be considered a derivative work, also protected under U.S. Copyright Law. It has since been updated and expanded for the written format.

This second edition has been fully revised, from cover to cover, to provide you with the latest information. But that's not all. Every important historical figure or landmark has been linked to additional online information to give you a way broader view of this magnificent city. The Kindle version has those links live, but the printed version includes a list at the end with all the links.

Finally, we've added 12 online videos covering most of the important locations mentioned in the book as well as additional links to other YouTube videos produced by us that complement the book's information. Those are also included at the end of the book.

All photographs included in this book are original works of art created by Orlando Mergal and are also registered separately at the U.S. Copyright Office.

Reproduction of this document, in part or in full, is prohibited.

Who Am I?

Orlando Mergal

Hi, my name is Orlando Mergal. I am a Content Creator, Blogger, Podcaster, Author, and New Media Expert. During 25 years I worked with the pharmaceutical, banking, insurance and service industries in Puerto Rico. Today I work on my own projects, including my Hablando De Tecnología podcast (*https://www.hablandodetecnologia.com*), which has over 370 episodes, Puerto Rico By GPS (*https://www.puertoricobygps.com*) a tourism blog that covers over 125 locations on the Island, and Puerto Rico Photography (*https://www.puertoricophotography.com*) an online gallery with over 1,000 fine art photographs of Puerto Rico and the U.S. National Parks.

I am totally bilingual and fluent in English and Spanish.

During my career I have worked with many of Puerto Rico's top executives delivering tailor-made communications tools for human resources, marketing and public relations. My business —Accurate Communications (*https://www,accuratecommunications.com*) — is a one-stop-shop for writing, translations, business publications, audiovisual and web related services.

I have authored six self-help DVDs, five books and produced countless audiovisual programs for my own projects and for my private clients.

Introduction

Welcome to the Old San Juan Walking Tour, the book for adventurous travelers who want to know it all about America's most beautiful city.

Following this book from start to finish will take about a day's walk. But before we proceed, let's start with a couple of guidelines.

You'll be walking along cobblestoned streets in a busy urban environment. Don't let yourself be distracted by the book's photos and entertaining nature. Pay attention to traffic at all times and be careful at intersections. Despite the world trend to convert old and medieval cities into pedestrian-friendly cities, the government of Old San Juan still allows vehicular traffic that destroys the city's delicate infrastructure. In fact, I recently published a video about this very situation. You can watch it here (*https://www.youtube.com/watch?v=ePLw1R4L9Ek*).

Contrary to what some people might believe, Old San Juan is actually a very safe city, with well-trained city police at almost every corner. However, like any other large metropolis, San Juan —and Puerto Rico as a whole— has its share of crime and violence. By following this book you assume the risks associated with its use and accept that neither "The Old San Juan Walking Tour", nor any of its representatives or publishers, will be held liable for injuries, accidents, arrests, or any other damages that you might suffer by using it.

The Old San Juan Walking Tour

You can also find information, pictures, audio, video and GPS maps for over 125 beautiful locations throughout Puerto Rico (including Old San Juan) at our website Puerto Rico By GPS.

Visit Puerto Rico By GPS at: https://www.puertoricobygps.com

This site was built using the latest "responsive design" technology, which means that no matter what portable device you bring with you (tablet or smartphone), as long as you're connected to the Internet, it will lead you straight to most popular attractions on the Island.

Finally, this edition includes 12 new videos, hosted at our private server, that illustrate many of the places mentioned in the book. You will find the links in the reference section at the end of the book.

It also includes detailed GPS maps for every chapter with color-coded markers and GPS coordinates. The link for that supplementary information is: **https://www.prxgps.com/mapsandvideos**.

Now read on and discover the many beautiful and interesting places that await you in Old San Juan.

Plaza Dársena to Paseo de La Princesa

Welcome once again to the Old San Juan Walking Tour, the book for adventurous travelers who want to know it all about America's most beautiful city. My name is Orlando Mergal and I've lived in Puerto Rico since 1963.

My parents, who were both Puerto Ricans, moved back to the Island when I was just 9 years old, so many of my teen and adult memories took place in the Old City. I'm also a landscape photographer, so all the pictures in this book were shot by me.

Founded in 1521 by Juan Ponce de León, San Juan is the oldest city under the American flag and the third oldest in the New World. Santo Domingo de Guzmán, the capital of the Dominican Republic to our west, was founded 23 years earlier in 1498 and holds the title of the oldest city in America. La Havana, Cuba was founded in 1515, making it the second oldest.

All three cities have been declared world heritage sites by the United Nations' Educational Scientific and Cultural Organization, better known as UNESCO.

Old San Juan is located on the northeastern coast of Puerto Rico, on a 47-square mile islet called "la isleta de San Juan", which is connected to the main island by the "Esteves", "San Antonio" and "Dos Hermanos" bridges.

Due to its privileged geographical location, the port of San Juan was used as a stopover for Spanish ships loaded with gold and silver from the Mexican "Situado". This also made the city a prime target for many of the foreign powers of the era that repeatedly tried to conquer it.

Some of the city's most famous attackers include: Sir Francis Drake in 1595, George Clifford (the Earl of Cumberland) in 1598 and Ralph Abercromby in 1797.

The Spanish knew very well that they needed to protect the city of San Juan from the attacks of pirates and foreign powers. Their first attempt came in 1533, when construction of the Palace of Santa Catalina (known today as "La Fortaleza", or Governor's Mansion) was started. However, the fort was constructed too far in and to the southeast, which left the entrance to the Bay unguarded.

Even before construction of "La Fortaleza" was finished Spanish engineers came to the realization that they would need to build an additional fort at a better location. Gonzalo Fernández de Oviedo, the acclaimed Spanish historiographer, reportedly said in 1537 "only blind men could have chosen such a poor spot for the fortification".

In 1540 construction of a small dome tower began at a headland located at the entrance to the bay. Two hundred and fifty years later the small tower had evolved into Fort San Felipe del Morro, a six-level military structure that protected the city for over 350 years. I've included a link to a YouTube video that I produced some years back about this fort.

To make matters worse for would-be attackers, in 1625 a small fortification known as the fort of San Juan de la Cruz (better known among the locals as "El Cañuelo") was constructed across the bay to trap hostile ships in a merciless crossfire.

Plaza Dársena to Paseo de La Princesa

In 1634 Spanish engineers saw the need to fortify the eastern side of the city to avoid land attacks, so they started the simultaneous construction of the city walls and Fort San Cristóbal. There's a link to my YouTube video about Fort San Cristóbal as well.

In 1785 both projects were completed. San Juan became a walled city and Fort San Cristóbal became the largest Spanish fortification in the New World; a true masterpiece of military engineering for the time.

La Fortaleza and San Juan Gate in the distance

For more than 100 years visitors arriving in San Juan would enter the city through one of 3 places. "Santiago Gate", on the east side, "España" or "San Justo Gate" on the south side or "San Juan Gate", on the western side. There are two additional gates through the wall but they lead out to the "Santa María Magdalena de Pazzi" cemetery on the north side.

In case you're curious, no one ever attempted to attack San Juan from the north. Why? Because there's a massive reef, that extends all the way from San Juan to the "Cangrejos" area in Isla Verde. Oh, and then there was the wall as well.

In 1897 government officials saw the need to expand the city to the east and the southeastern quadrant of the city wall (including

The Old San Juan Walking Tour

the España and Santiago gates), as well as a substantial part of fort San Cristóbal, were demolished. Even so, the remaining portion of Fort San Cristóbal is still the largest Spanish fortification built in the new world.

Our walk will start at the southern coast of the old city, at a small square known as "Plaza Dársena", a few steps to the west of pier 1. If you are visiting the Island on a cruise ship please walk west along the waterfront until you reach the small square next to Pier 1. This present day waterfront was where cargo ships arriving at the Island wood dock to enter the city through the España (or San Justo) gate.

If you arrived on the island by plane please have your taxi driver drop you off at "Plaza Dársena". Taxis are readily available all over the city, so you'll easily catch a cab back to your hotel after a day of beautiful sites.

The word "dársena" means inner harbor or dock, which is exactly what it was during the city's Spanish colonial period. Ships arriving in 18th century San Juan would dock at "la dársena", which was surrounded by a small square followed by the city wall and the España gate.

Standing at "Plaza Dársena", with your back towards the water, you'll see the old Banco Popular building in front of you towards the left and the south side of the old US Post Office and Federal Court building to your right.

For many years the Banco Popular building in Old San Juan was the tallest structure on the Island. Today, one of the tallest buildings on the Island also belongs to Banco Popular, but it's a 22-story building located in the Hato Rey commercial district.

Another interesting fact involves the US Post Office and Federal Court building on your right. For many years the building was the only one in Puerto Rico with a heating system. Somehow, U.S. engineers got it wrong and installed a heating system on an Island that averages 80° Fahrenheit a year.

Plaza Dársena to Paseo de La Princesa

Straight across from "Plaza Dársena", in front of the Banco Popular building, there's a small square dedicated to 19th century Puerto Rican educator and independence advocate Eugenio María de Hostos. This is exactly where the San Justo gate stood during the 18th and 19th centuries.

Visitors arriving at the Old City by ship would go through San Justo gate onto San Justo street, which is the one on the right of the Banco Popular tower, when looking from "Plaza Dársena".

If you look a little to your left you'll spot a sentry box where the city wall ends today. This marks the entrance to the "Paseo de La Princesa", a long promenade that leads to the old city's colonial jailhouse.

Many Saturdays and Sundays this area is filled with pushcart vendors carrying the best in Puerto Rican crafts. Today "La Princesa" is a beautiful gray and white structure that houses the Puerto Rico Tourism Company's central office.

This brings us to the end of chapter 1 of the Old San Juan Walking Tour. Our next chapter will start at "La Princesa" promenade and take us to the entrance to "Paseo del Morro".

If you enjoy this book please take a minute and write us a brief review on Amazon. And don't forget to visit Puerto Rico By GPS where you'll find additional information, pictures, audio, videos and GPS maps for every attraction in Old San Juan.

Finally, if you love the beach, don't forget to check out my other book: "Puerto Rico Beach By Beach" where you will find detailed information about Puerto Rico's most wonderful beaches. The link is also in the reference section.

Paseo de La Princesa to Plaza de la Rogativa

The "Paseo de La Princesa" has existed since Spanish colonial times, but the one you see today was rebuilt in 1992 to commemorate the 500th anniversary of the discovery of America.

The event was highlighted by the Columbus Regatta, which brought the world's largest tall ships to the port of San Juan. Many of the city's buildings, monuments and plazas were brought up to date or rebuilt for the occasion.

"Paseo de la Princesa" / La Princesa Promenade

As we walk down "Paseo de La Princesa" we will be bordering the city wall. You will recall from the previous chapter that construction of the city wall started in 1634. By 1650 the walls protected the north, west and southern sides of the city, while a half-built Fort San Cristóbal protected the eastern side from land attacks.

The walls average a height of 42 feet. Thickness goes from 18 feet at the top to 40 feet at the bottom. They're made of solid sandstone blocks held together with mortar, limestone, sand and water. However, in order to resist the impact of a 20-pound canon ball, traveling at great velocity, the walls were constructed following a "sandwich" design where the exterior and interior layers of the wall are made of solid sandstone and the center is filled with impact-absorbing rubblework.

If a canon ball managed to pierce the outer layer, the energy-absorbing core would stop the projectile. It would've been like striking a pillow.

Felisa Rincón de Gautier Statue

You will also notice that the promenade is lined with gardens, a small park for children and statues along the base of the city wall. One particularly interesting statue —near the entrance of the promenade— is dedicated to Felisa Rincón de Gautier, better known as "Doña Fela", who was the first woman to hold the office of mayor of a capitol city in the western hemisphere. She served for a period of 22 years from 1946 to 1968.

"Doña Fela" is best remembered by the "sanjuaneros" for

Paseo de La Princesa to Plaza de la Rogativa

bringing a planeload of snow for the city's disadvantaged children to play in during Christmas season. But her many achievements earned her accolates, awards, commendations and degrees from most of the world's leading countries.

In 1954 she was recognized as "Woman Of The Americas" by the Union of American Women of New York for her many contributions to the western hemisphere.

The statue shows "Doña Fela" in her traditional attire, which always included a wig and Spanish fan from here extensive collection.

Many of "Doña Fela's" belongings are on exhibition at the Felisa Rincón de Gautier Museum located on the corner of "Caleta de San Juan" and "Clara Lair" streets, right behind San Juan Gate. You'll be walking right past it in a couple of minutes.

This was once the smallest apartment in the world.

And here's a piece of trivia for you. Did you know that "doña Fela" was never actually the mayor of San Juan? The fact is that the position didn't exist when she was elected. Her formal title was "city manager". The first person to hold the position of Mayor of San Juan was actually Carlos Romero Barceló, who was elected in November of 1968.

After you pass the statues look closely towards the base of the city wall, you'll see the sealed-off entrances to many tunnels. Legend has it that many of those tunnels run under the city linking many of its fortifications. Of course, city officials deny it.

Right before you reach "La Princesa" you will see a gate on your right and a gazebo near the base of the city wall. If you look carefully over the city wall you will see a very small building painted in yellow. For many years it held the Guinness World Record as the world's smallest apartment. Today nobody lives there. So I guess you can't call it an apartment anymore.

This brings us to "La Princesa", a beautiful colonial building painted in gray and white that houses the central office of the Puerto Rico Tourism Company. Don't let the inviting looks of this restored structure fool you. In colonial times this was one of the most feared prisons in the Caribbean.

"La Princesa" / Puerto Rico Tourism Company

The building was constructed in 1837 and operated as a penitentiary until 1960. More than 240 prisoners were held behind bars at "La Princesa" and many were hanged there.

After the United States invaded the Island in 1898 the jailhouse held many famous Puerto Rican nationalists, including world-renowned poets Juan Antonio Corretjer and Antonio Matos Paoli. Nationalist leader Pedro Albizu Campos lived most of his last days in this prison and it was rumored that he was subjected to experimentation with radiation. He died a cruel and painful death on April 21, 1965.

Paseo de La Princesa to Plaza de la Rogativa

In 1994, under the administration of President Bill Clinton, the Department of Energy revealed that it had, in fact, conducted radiation experiments on human beings. These experiments were carried out, without the consent or knowledge of the prisoners, during the 1950s to 1970s, and Pedro Albizu Campos was reportedly one of those victims.

"La Princesa" has a beautifully restored lobby and courtyard as well as modern art exhibitions that you are sure to enjoy.

Our walk continues towards the "Raíces" fountain, which is located at the far end of the "Paseo de la Princesa". If you look towards your upper right, over the city wall, just before you reach the fountain, you will see the "Siervas de María" monastery, an impressive colonial structure perched over the corner of the city wall.

"Yaíces" Fountain

The "Raíces" fountain was unveiled on May 30, 1992 to commemorate the 500th anniversary of the discovery of America and to inaugurate the newly restored "La Princesa" Promenade. The fountain is comprised of human figures representing the Island's Taíno, Spanish and African heritage.

You will also notice a series of concrete pillars surrounding the fountain. These used to hold a brass chain about three times the thickness of a grown man's arm. Well, the chain is no longer there and only one of the pillars still has the brass ring where the chain used to go. How it disappeared, I don't know. What's really puzzling is that this is one of the most guarded areas in the entire city. There's always a policeman somewhere near. So how did this chain disappear? Hmmmm.

"Paseo del Morro" / "El Morro" Promenade

After passing the "Raíces" fountain you will make a slight right and walk onto another promenade that extends alongside the city wall all the way to Fort San Felipe del Morro. Don't let the tree-covered entrance fool you if you decide to walk the entire promenade. At a normal pace it will take you at least an hour to walk the entire promenade. Oh, and the only trees you'll see are the ones at the very beginning of your walk and the ones next to San Juan Gate.

The walk is beautiful and interesting, but make sure to wear comfortable shoes, a wide brim hat, use a healthy amount of sunblock and take along a couple of bottles of water. This kind of walk can be quite exhausting under the burning Puerto Rican sun.

Paseo de La Princesa to Plaza de la Rogativa

Right after you walk onto this second promenade you will find a small park on your right with modern sculptures that look like iron spears extending into the heavens. The sculptures were created by Carmen Inés Blondet, a San Juan born artist who is best known for her public art. The pieces were unveiled in 1996 by the Puerto Rico Tourism Company.

After you emerge from under the tree cover you will be walking alongside the city wall and immediately below the "Palace of Santa Catalina". As you will recall from our first chapter, this building is known today as "La Fortaleza" and has served for centuries as the Governor's Mansion. The building was expanded and remodeled in 1846, which gave it the palatial appearance that it has today. Tours are conducted in English and Spanish and must be reserved in advance. Contrary to other palaces around the world, La Fortaleza is the working residence of the Governor of Puerto Rico, so excursions can be unexpectedly cancelled due to state activities. For more information, please call 787-721-7000. Suitable attire is always required.

After you pass La Fortaleza the promenade turns slightly to the right and you'll see San Juan Gate a few hundred feet in front of you. In colonial times, passenger ships arriving at San Juan harbor would anchor outside San Juan Gate and smaller boats would bring the people to shore. From there, arriving visitors would walk up "La Caleta de San Juan" –which is the street immediately behind San Juan Gate– and go straight to San Juan Cathedral to thank the Lord for a safe voyage.

Before reaching San Juan Gate there is still another tree-covered plaza honoring Isabel de Trastamara, the catholic queen of Spain that was so instrumental in funding Christopher Columbus in his voyage of discovery.

Our walk will take us through San Juan Gate and onto a small square known as "La Plaza de la Rogativa'. But before you enter the Gate take a look along the remainder of the promenade. It's a great place to take pictures and —if you prefer— you can close your book and continue straight down the promenade until you reach the base of Fort San Felipe del Morro. City authorities have plans to extend this promenade all around the city, but as it is today, you'll have to turn back at El Morro and enter the city through San Juan Gate.

"La Puerta de San Juan" / San Juan Gate

Before entering San Juan Gate notice the inscription above the entrance that reads "Benedictus Oui Venit In Nomine Domini". It's Latin for: "Welcome those who come in the name of God", a testament to the city's Catholic heritage.

After entering San Juan Gate you will reach the intersection of two streets. La Caleta de San Juan, which is the one entering the city and "Clara Lair" Street which leads left or right from where you stand. You will also notice a pink colonial building on the intersection of Caleta de San Juan and Clara Lair. This used to be the residence of the late mayor of San Juan Felisa Rincón de Gautier. Today the building is a museum dedicated to our beloved "Doña Fela". Feel free to visit it and learn all about the many accomplishments of this outstanding woman. Admission is free!

Right next to the entrance of San Juan Gate you will notice a narrow tree-covered uphill walkway on your left hand side that extends diagonally alongside Clara Lair Street. It leads to "La Plaza de la Rogativa" which would loosely translate as "Procession Square".

Paseo de La Princesa to Plaza de la Rogativa

The sculpture in the center of the square was commissioned in 1971 by a group of Puerto Rican businessmen to commemorate Ralph Abercromby's failed siege of the City. After failing to take San Juan in 1797, the British Leutenant-General ordered a naval

"La Rogativa" Statue

blockade to cut off Spanish reinforcements. After witnessing for weeks the anguish of his troops and citizens, the Spanish governor called for a procession or "rogativa" to implore for divine intervention. The women of San Juan organized a procession and marched through the streets carrying torches and rustic instruments. Apparently, Abercromby mistook the procession for the arrival of Spanish reinforcements and fled the Island fearing that he would be outnumbered.

"La Plaza de la Rogativa" offers an excellent view of the northwestern side of the Palace of Santa Catalina as well as the portion of the city wall leading to Fort San Felipe del Morro.

If you enjoy this book please take a minute and write us a brief review at Amazon. And don't forget to visit Puerto Rico By GPS where you'll find additional information, pictures, audio, videos and GPS maps to every attraction in Old San Juan.

Plaza de la Rogativa to Fort San Felipe del Morro

Our fourth chapter starts at "Plaza de la Rogativa" a beautiful square that commemorates Ralph Abercromby's failed attempt to take the city of San Juan in 1797.

Standing at la Plaza de la Rogativa, with your back towards the bay, you will see la Caleta de las Monjas, a narrow street half-paved in cobblestone that leads to El Convento Hotel and San Juan Cathedral to the right and towards Fort San Felipe del Morro to the left. This segment of our walk will take us to Fort San Felipe del Morro, as well as to other interesting sights on the western tip of Islet.

When leaving la Plaza de la Rogativa we will walk through the iron gates at the northwestern end of the plaza. As we walk northwest, towards Fort San Felipe del Morro, we will be bordering the southwestern side of "La Casa Blanca", a white washed stucco dwelling, built in 1521 to serve as the official residence of governor Juan Ponce de León. The governor never lived there, but his family made it their official residence until de 18th Century.

After a few minutes you'll come to a fork in the road and you'll see a colonial structure painted in bright pink. It's called "La Casa Rosada" or Pink House, and it was built in 1812 to house the Spanish soldiers that guarded the nearby San Agustín Bastion. Later on, in 1851, it was converted into the Spanish Army's

"La Casa Rosa" / The Pink House

officer's quarters. In more recent times, the building served as a museum of Puerto Rican Arts and Crafts, as the headquarters of the Puerto Rico Architects Association and even as a daycare center for the children of the city's government employees. Today it is closed and serves no particular purpose.

Across the street from "La Casa Rosada" you will see a sentry box that points straight to the San Juan Gate and "La Fortaleza" area. This is an excellent spot for taking beautiful pictures of

View of "La Fortaleza" (the governor's mansion) and San Juan Gate

these historical landmarks. But, PLEASE be extra careful if you are visiting the Island with children, and refrain from walking on the city walls. The 40-foot fall onto the solid concrete surface of the Paseo del Morro below will surely ruin your day.

Our walk will continue northwest along the left side of the fork. Immediately after we pass "La Casa Rosada" you will see a couple of tennis courts on your right and a large green plot of land on your left, with a huge tree in the center. In Spanish colonial times this used to be the San Agustín Bastion.

Bastions were semi polygonal projecting structures, equipped with heavy artillery, that were erected at frequent intervals along the walls. They were designed to take advantage of the local topography. Rounded sentry boxes at various corners served as observation posts to guard the city wall.

"Polvorín" / Powder House

After leaving the San Agustín Bastion we will continue along the city wall until we reach one of the city's only two remaining powder houses. You will recognize the structure because it has two very tall chimneys, one at each end of the building. Powder houses had special air ducts that ran along the building's walls and connected to the chimneys. This created a vacuum that kept the building cool and dry to avoid accidental explosions.

Immediately to the left of the powder house you will find the Santa Elena Bastion, where you can still see the base where the heavy artillery used to sit. If you look towards the entrance of the bay you will notice that it's quite narrow. You will also see Fort San Juan de la Cruz, sitting across the bay right next to the entrance. Now, imagine what it must've been like to navigate through this crossfire nightmare in the 18th Century.

Bastión de Santa Elena / "Santa Elena" Bastion

Walking uphill along the fence, about a hundred steps from the Santa Elena Bastion, we reach the remains of the San Fernando Bastion, which still has the original rails where the large Spanish canons used to sit. This bastion guarded the southwestern corner of the dry moat that protected the entrance to Fort San Felipe del Morro.

The fence ends before reaching the moat so PLEASE be extra careful if you have small children in your party.

Our walk will continue bordering Fort San Felipe del Morro until we reach a small bridge that leads to the entrance. In colonial times this bridge had a section that was actually a drawbridge, right next to its huge doors, which protected the eastern side of the fort. Attacking forces arriving from the east would've been met by a dry moat surrounding the fort that would've forced them to descend (with their backs towards the fort) before attempting to climb the fort walls.

Fort "San Felipe del Morro"

This gave the Spanish forces several advantages. First, the moat would've protected the base of the fort walls from enemy canon fire, something that never occurred. Second, while climbing down into the moat, the attacking foot soldiers would've been sitting ducks for the Spanish forces. If you're interested in the inner workings of this magnificent fort there's a video on YouTube I published several years ago that explains them in great detail. The link is in the reference section.

Visiting Fort San Felipe del Morro used to be free, but several years ago the National Park Service decided to charge a small fee to help cover the fort's maintenance and ongoing restoration. The $10 entrance fee is actually a bargain. And if you're also planning to visit Fort San Cristóbal –which we strongly recommend– it will cover them both for the same price during a 24-hour period.

Entering Fort San Felipe del Morro is like stepping back in time. Once you pass the fort's massive entrance you'll find yourself in the main courtyard and you'll see a tunnel shaped ramp that leads straight down towards the Santa Barbara battery. Immediately to the right, before entering the tunnel shaped ramp, there's a small concession stand with all sorts of books and memorabilia about the forts, Old San Juan and Puerto Rico in general.

Gunnery Ramp

Now you'll have to make a decision. Are you going to explore the fort from the top down or from the bottom up? Personally, I prefer to go from the bottom up because you'll be less tired at the beginning, which is when you'll be doing most of the climbing.

Now that we have that out the way, lets start down the tunnel shaped ramp towards the Santa Barbara battery level. Once again, if you have children in your party, please hold them firmly while you walk down the steps. DO NOT attempt to walk down the center ramp. One missed step and you'll roll down the ramp faster than a Spanish cannon ball. By the way, this ramp was called the Main Artillery Ramp and it was used to move canons weighing up to 10,000 pounds and other military equipment using a sophisticated rope and pulley system called a "block and tackle".

Once we reach the Santa Barbara battery level we'll take the next staircase leading down towards the lower patio. Right next to the base of this staircase you will find a passageway on your left that leads to another downward ramp. This ramp leads to the interior of the original 1539 tower that's covered by the Santa Barbara battery today. After walking down this ramp you'll be standing under the dome of the original tower, which has several interesting features of its own.

Looking to your left you will see yet another set of stairs. It leads towards the first level Water Battery Area. The last time that I visited the fort this staircase was closed due to personnel constraints. Like its name implies, the artillery in the Water Battery Area would shoot red-hot canon balls at the waterline of enemy ships. The enormous force of these projectiles, and the high temperature at which they were fired, would pierce the ship's hull, start a fire and allow seawater to pour in.

At the opposite end of the tower you'll see the closed-off longholes from the original structure. Sentries guarding the tower could shoot their muskets and retreat through the narrow tunnel, from where they could reload safely under cover.

A memory from the Spanish-American War

On the upper right quadrant of the tower dome there is still another piece of history from the fort's turbulent past. But in this case it's a real piece. If you look carefully you'll see a metal fragment sticking out of the dome structure. On May 12, 1898, a month after the United States declared war on Spain, a US naval squadron commanded by Admiral William T. Sampson attacked the city of San Juan for nearly three consecutive hours. El Morro's defenses were hit with several hundred shells, one of which pierced through the original tower dome.

After walking back up the ramp we'll arrive at the lower patio. Looking directly under the staircase you will see two large arches directly below the main artillery ramp. The one on the left was the fort's kitchen and the one on the right was the forge. On the opposite side of the patio are the casemates or gunrooms. The guns in these rooms pointed straight out to sea and their mission was to shoot at the hulls and decks of enemy ships. Their enclosed nature made them practically indestructible.

El Morro's Defense Systems

At the center of the lower patio there's a circular staircase that leads to the fourth level. If you wish, you can go up this staircase or you can use the wider one that we took on the way down. Either way, you will end up right next to the Santa Barbara Battery.

Several years ago you could still see one of the original breech-loading rifled guns that defended el Morro against enemy attackers. Now the Santa Barbara Battery is only a concrete promon-

Plaza de la Rogativa to Fort San Felipe del Morro

tory were you can shoot a selfie and you'll have an excellent view of the San Juan de la Cruz fort, sitting across de bay. You'll also see an occasional cruise ship arriving at or leaving San Juan.

Standing at the Santa Barbara Battery, with you back towards the sea, you will notice the V-shaped design of Fort San Felipe del Morro. On both sides you will see the empty openings were the fort's guns used to sit.

Actually, if you observe the fort straight from above, you'll discover that it resembles the head of a bull.

Walking towards your left along the fourth level gun area you will find another circular staircase that leads to the fifth level Carmen Battery, which supported the Santa Barbara Battery. These guns pointed towards the entire northwestern sector of Old San Juan.

Directly across the Carmen Battery there's a small ramp that goes up around the fort's lighthouse to the Ochoa half-bastion and the Austria half-bastion. These half bastions form the horns of the bull that we mentioned a few paragraphs back. Both half bastions are linked together by a straight wall that sits directly over the fort entrance. This entire area protected the rear side of the fort in the event of a land attack.

When exiting El Morro you'll probably be struck by the barren appearance of the fort grounds. The Spaniards called this a glacis or "emplanada" and the purpose was to deny attacking forces any possible cover from the fort's gunners and musketeers. Today, the only ones baking in the sun are civilians.

From here our walk will take us straight into the old city following the trail that leads away from the fort. But if you prefer, you can walk alongside the city wall on your left and return to the trail were it ends next to the Colonial Sanitarium. You'll catch a stunning view of the Old San Juan Cemetery, as well as the north side of the city wall and seafront. We DO NOT however recommend that you venture alone into the cemetery grounds. Once again, PLEASE refrain from walking on the city walls. We'd like to have you around for the remainder of this walk.

If you enjoy this book please take a minute and write us a brief review on Amazon. And don't forget to visit Puerto Rico By GPS where you'll find additional information, pictures, audio, videos and GPS maps to every attraction in Old San Juan.

Finally, if you love the beach, don't forget to check out my other book: "Puerto Rico Beach By Beach" where you'll find detailed information about Puerto Rico's most wonderful beaches. The link is in the reference section.

Colonial Sanitarium to Plaza San José

Our fifth chapter starts at the Colonial Sanitarium, a beautiful structure built in 1854, by royal decree, to serve as an asylum for the mentally insane. The building's red dome roof stands out from the El Morro grounds and the opposite end of the Glacis. Its twin courtyards used to be adorned with luscious gardens and fountains that added charm and ambiance.

After the US invasion in 1898, the Colonial Sanitarium was converted into the Fort Brooke Military Reservation Army Barracks. Fort Brooke was a military complex that operated under the U.S. Department of the Army and included Fort San Felipe del Morro, Fort San Cristóbal, Fort San Juan de la Cruz (better know as El Cañuelo), the 19th Century military barracks of Ballajá, the Colonial Sanitarium and several other adjacent structures.

In 1949 the San Juan National Historic Site was established and the entire complex was transferred to the Department of the Interior. However, the facilities were actually in Army hands until September of 1961. Many of the structures surrounding the Colonial Sanitarium remained closed and abandoned until 1992, when Puerto Rico celebrated the Quincentennial of the Discovery of America.

In 1965 the old Sanitarium became the Puerto Rican Academy of Fine Arts. Today the building looks clean and many times the student's projects take up much of what used to be the building's courtyards and fountains. Most tourists walk by without a hint of the building's history.

Ballajá Military Barracks and Colonial Sanitarium

Right behind the colonial Sanitarium there's another building that attracts almost no tourist traffic. It was built in the 1840's by the Spanish colonial government to be the "Asilo de Beneficencia" or "home of the poor". Its architecture inspires an austere feeling that's compounded by its silent atmosphere. Two beautiful interior courtyards add charm and elegance to this immense structure. Most recently it housed the offices of the Puerto Rico Institute of Culture, but as far as I know it's presently closed.

Across the street from the Asilo de Beneficencia is a huge colonial structure painted in light brown with tan trim known as the "Cuartel de Ballajá" or Ballajá Military Barracks. In colonial times this building housed over 1,000 Spanish soldiers along with their wives and children in the typical austere setting of an Iberian monastery.

Construction began in 1854 and the main building was completed in 1863. Later on, a separate chapel was added in 1881. That chapel no longer exists. The "Cuartel de Ballajá" is a three-story structure with large entrances at opposite ends and arched balconies surrounding an immense courtyard that covers the building's water reservoir.

The "Cuartel de Ballajá" was the largest building constructed by the Spaniards in the New World. It was also the last. After the US invasion in 1898, the building became the headquarters of the US Army's Infantry division and part of the Fort Brooke Military Reservation. In 1943 it was converted into a military medical facility known as the Rodríguez Hospital.

In 1992, the building's restoration was completed and the second floor became the permanent home of the "Museum of the Americas". The museum features itinerating exhibits, as well as an outstanding collection of Caribbean and European American arts and crafts. Whatever you do, don't leave without enjoying the outstanding collection of carved saints, a tradition of excellence among the Island's leading artisans. The museum is open Monday thru Friday, from 10:00 in the morning to 4:00 in the afternoon. On Saturdays and Sundays, it opens from 11:00 in the morning to 5:00 in the afternoon. Admission is $6 for adults and $4 for children.

Another attraction at the Ballajá Military Barracks is the Pablo Casals Museum, dedicated to the renown Spanish cellist Pablo Casals.

Pablo Casals came to Puerto Rico in 1956, in the midst of the Spanish Civil War, and lived on the Island –where his mother and wife had been born– until his death in 1973. His legacy includes the world famous Casals Festival, the Puerto Rico Symphony Orchestra, The Puerto Rico Conservatory of Music and the Children's Special Strings Program.

His cello and piano are on display at the museum as well as many of his medals and commendations from countries around the world.

As you continue up the street between the "Asilo de Beneficencia" and the "Cuartel de Ballajá" you'll arrive at the "Plaza de los Niños", a small square dedicated in 1998 to nineteenth century Puerto Rican educator and independence advocate Eugenio María de Hostos "Citizen of the Americas", in behalf of the children of a grateful motherland. The square is adorned with a beautiful statue that evokes "de Hostos" surrounded by children in a cheerful atmosphere.

"Plaza de los Niños" dedicated to Dr. José Celso Barbosa

Sadly, the photo above is not an honest rendition of the square. I arrived at this image after nearly 8 hours of Photoshop work to remove trash and grafitti. However, I will admit that today its in way better condition. The only thing missing would be some landscaping and flowers.

A few steps further up the street we'll arrive at the oldest continuously occupied residence in the Western Hemisphere. In 1521, the Spanish colonial government started construction of "La Casa Blanca" or white house to be the official residence of governor Juan Ponce de León. It was also the Island's first stone fort (remember, construction of La Fortaleza started in 1533).

The governor died that same year in Cuba, after being mortally wounded while attempting to establish a colony near the Caloosahatchee River in Florida. The Ponce de León family occupied La Casa Blanca for over 250 years until the Spanish military took over the facilities in 1779. After the US invasion in 1998, the Casa Blanca became the official residence of the US Military Commanders until it was returned to the people of Puerto Rico in 1966.

"La Casa Blanca"

Two stone lions and the family's coat of arms over the massive wooden doors adorn the entrance to this beautiful building. The white stucco dwelling is comprised of a foyer, study, two bedrooms, a dining room,

"La Casa Blanca" Gardens and Fountain

kitchen, oratorio, garden, orchard, and a special throne room for receiving royal visits.

Today the complex serves as a National Historic Monument and houses a museum about life on the Island during the 16th, 17th and 18th Centuries. Each room is decorated using antique Spanish furniture to represent the building's different historical periods as authentically as possible.

One special feature is the garden fountain, which was inspired on the famous Alhambra castle in Granada, Spain.

After exiting La Casa Blanca we will continue straight on Calle San Sebastián. Please note that all streets in Old San Juan are one way, with the exception of Norzagaray Street, so in this case we will in fact be walking against traffic. Immediately after we pass "La Plaza de los Niños" we will see the old colonial hospital "Nuestra Señora de la Concepción" painted in mustard yellow on our left. For years the building was a run down structure. However, it was remodeled and became the Plastic Arts School.

Immediately after passing the old colonial hospital we will see a narrow alley on our right that leads down to "Calle Sol". This alley is known as "el Callejón del Hospital" (the alley of the hospital) and it has served as inspiration for painters and photographers. Today, it takes a little more editing and imagination to create a great picture here, due to its present condition.

The next building on the left after passing "El Callejón del Hospital" is "La Liga del Arte", a non-profit organization that has been the training place for many of the Island's finest artists. "La Liga del Arte" offers classes for small children as well as adults and all proceeds are used to further the organization's noble cause.

After passing "La Liga del Arte" we arrive at the intersection of "Calle San Sebastián" and "Calle Cristo". By now you must've noticed that I'm using the word "Calle" instead of the word street, and that the term precedes the name of the street as opposed to English, where it follows the name. I thought it actually would be easier to call things by their actual name, instead of translating them into something unintelligible.

You see, in Spanish you have calles, caletas and callejones, which loosely translates into streets, short streets and alleys. It would be easy to refer to "Calle Cristo" as Cristo Street, but it wouldn't be as easy to refer to "La Caleta de Las Monjas" as the Nun's Short Street. So in the name of simplicity and clarity, we'll stick to the original Spanish names.

At the corner of "Calle San Sebastián" and "Calle Cristo" you'll see the famous Plaza San José, where the "Fiestas de la Calle San Sebastián" take place every year on the third week of January. This hasn't been the case since 2019 due to the Covid-19 pandemic, but I sure expect to see them back someday.

Puerto Ricans love to party and Puerto Rico has one of the longest Christmas seasons in the world (if not the longest). It all starts on Thanksgiving Day, as the turkey dinner tradition takes on a

"Cabezudos"

Latin flavor of its own. Many families literally bring home their turkey in one hand and their Christmas tree and ornaments in the other. Often while the turkey is roasting away in the oven, the family will be busy decorating the Christmas tree. From there on, the Christmas season extends for approximately seven weeks and it concludes with the "Fiestas de La Calle San Sebastián".

This hasn't always been this way. In Spanish colonial times, Christmas season started on the 24th of December with "La Nochebuena" or Christmas Eve. This marked the night before the birth of our Lord Jesus Christ. From there the period extended to January 6, when the most important festivity, El Día de Los Reyes Magos" or Three Kings Day" was celebrated.

In 1898, the United States invaded Puerto Rico and brought along Thanksgiving Day and Santa Claus. Now, don't forget, Puerto Ricans love to Party. So now we had this new bird —that we learned to stuff with plantains and garlic— and a chubby guy, in a red and white suit, with no chimneys to climb into. So how do you make the best of that? ¡You party!

Then father Madrazo (the parish priest at San Jose Church) came along in 1954 and organized the first "Fiestas de la Calle San Sebastián" as a fundraiser for his parish and to restore many of the deteriorated structures on the street. One thing led to another and the organizers decided to include the famous "cabezudos", which originally wore giant masks representing the Spanish monarchs Fernando and Isabel, and marched down the street alongside residents and participants.

Today the "cabezudos" represent many characters derived from Puerto Rican folklore and march down the street followed by a "comparsa" and thousands of participants. A "comparsa" is a small musical group that generally includes several plenera drums, güiros and maracas.

But the "Fiestas de la Calle San Sebastián" go way beyond the "cabezudos" parade. The four-day event features artisan fairs, chess

"Cabezudos"

matches, folkloric events and concerts under the stars. The religious aspect is kept alive by a procession in honor of the patron saint and a mass that's traditionally celebrated on Saturday evening.

If you enjoy this book please take a minute and write us a brief review at Amazon. And don't forget to visit Puerto Rico By GPS where you'll find additional information, pictures, audio, videos and GPS maps to every attraction in Old San Juan.

Finally, if you love the beach, don't forget to check out my other book: "Puerto Rico Beach By Beach" where you will find detailed information about Puerto Rico's most wonderful beaches. The link is in the reference section.

Plaza San José to San Juan Museum

Our sixth chapter starts at Plaza San Jose, the beautiful square where the famous Fiestas de la Calle San Sebastián take place every year on the third week of January.

Right in the middle of Plaza San Jose, there's a statue dedicated to Spanish Conquistador, and the Island's first governor, Juan Ponce de León. The statue faces west, which was the direction in which he headed on his final voyage in search of the Fountain of

"Plaza San José" / Juan Ponce de León Statue

Youth. The metal for this statue reportedly came from the melted canons and guns recovered from the English ships destroyed during a failed attack on Fort El Morro in the 16th Century.

The Statue was originally placed at "Plaza de Santiago" which stood behind the now demolished Santiago Gate. On January 23rd 1894 it was replaced by the now famous Christopher Columbus statue and that plaza was renamed as Plaza Colón. Since then, the statue of Juan Ponce de León has adorned the beautiful Plaza San José.

Right next to the statue of Juan Ponce de León is San José Church, a beautiful whitewashed structure built in the 16th century. The temple was closed for close to 20 years to undergo restoration. It was reopened to the public in 2021.

"Convento de los Dominicos" / Dominican Convent

San José Church is one of the few gothic churches in the New World. Construction started in 1530 after governor Juan Ponce de León donated the land to build San José Square, the temple and the Dominican Convent next door.

The church's gothic architecture is breathtaking. Puerto Rico's most famous painter José Campeche is reportedly buried at "Iglesia San José", as was originally Juan Ponce de León.

The wooden crucifix hanging over the church's altar was donated by Ponce de León in the 16th Century. And the 15th Century altar was built to order in Cadiz, Spain.

The fact that the church had never been restored was both a blessing and a challenge. The immense amount of work and resources that were required to return the structure to its original splendor was beyond imagination. But the fact that it had never been touched also made things easier from the restoration standpoint.

San José Church is by no means the oldest church in San Juan. That honor goes to San Juan Cathedral that predates it by a few years and is probably the oldest cathedral in the New World. However, the original San Juan Cathedral was destroyed by a hurricane and the present day building only dates back to the 1800's.

Next door to San José Church is the "Convento de los Dominicos" or the Dominican Convent, that is a contemporary structure built in the 1530's. In fact, San José Church was originally the chapel for the Dominican Convent and was originally named the Church of "Santo Tomás de Aquino". It was given its present day name when the Jesuits took over the facilities in 1865.

The Dominican Convent was the first convent in Puerto Rico. It was established 1523 by the Dominican friars. It also provided shelter for the city's women and children during many Caribbean attacks. In 1865 the Jesuits took over the Convent, shortly after the Spanish government closed down the building. After the US invasion in 1898, the US Army used the building as its headquarters until 1966.

Today the building belongs to the Puerto Rico Institute of Culture and is in a sad state of disrepair. It houses a small chapel museum on the first floor that displays religious objects and many fine pieces of art. The building's center courtyard and 16th Century architecture alone make it a worthwhile visit.

A little to the west of the Convento De Los Domincos is a modern sqaure that was built in 1992 to commemorate the Quincentennial of the Discovery of America. It's called "La Plaza del Quinto Centenario" and it sits between the Convento de los Dominicos and the Cuartel de Ballajá that we discussed during the last segment.

"Tótem Telúrico"

In the center of the square there's a huge modern sculpture, by renown local artist Jaime Suárez, that is known among the locals as the "Totem Telúrico". On weekends the plaza is usually filled with teenagers on skates and children enjoying the walk-in water fountain at the lower end next to Norzagaray Street. The plaza also offers an excellent view of the Old San Juan Cemetery, el Morro Grounds and many other adjacent structures.

When you reach the lower end of the plaza –facing towards the ocean– you will be looking at Norzagaray street. This street goes from the El Morro grounds to Fort San Cristóbal at the opposite end of the city. We will not be going to Fort San Cristóbal just yet, but we will be walking in that direction until we reach "El Museo de San Juan", a beautiful colonial structure painted mustard and light yellow with white trimming that's located immediately after the "Convento de los Dominicos".

The building was inaugurated on January 18, 1857 as the colonial city's farmer's market. After the US invasion in 1898, the building became a military warehouse during World War II. After the war ended, the building returned to its original function and later became the home of the now defunct "División de la Comunidad", which promoted socio-educational and cultural events.

In 1979 it became the San Juan Museum of Art & History. In 1989, the building was severely damaged by Hurricane Hugo and became an abandoned structure. On September 28, 1993 the building was reopened as the San Juan Museum.

The museum has an interactive exhibition that covers over 500 years of San Juan and Puerto Rican history. It also presents itinerating exhibits and frequently stages events at its beautiful center courtyard.

When exiting the museum on Norzagaray we will be walking briefly towards el Morro grounds until we reach the corner of the building. Now you will need to make a decision. You can walk back the way you came until you reach Plaza San José or you can walk around the San Juan Museum building and reach Calle San Sebastián. If you decide to do the later, turn left at the corner of the building, left again at the end of the street and immediately turn right at the first corner. You will now be standing on Calle del Mercado, which would loosely translate into Market Street.

San Juan Museum

The green doors right behind you were in fact the original entrance to the colonial farmer's market built in 1857. At the end of

Calle del Mercado you reach the intersection with Calle San Sebastian and you will once again turn right which will lead you back to Plaza San Jose and the corner of Calle Cristo and Calle San Sebastián.

If you enjoy this book please take a minute and write us a brief review at Amazon. And don't forget to visit Puerto Rico By GPS where you'll find additional information, pictures, audio, videos and GPS maps to every attraction in Old San Juan.

Finally, if you love the beach, don't forget to check out my other book: "Puerto Rico Beach By Beach" where you will find detailed information about Puerto Rico's most wonderful beaches. The link is in the reference section.

Plaza San José to Parque de las Palomas

Our seventh chapter starts at the corner of Calle Cristo and Calle San Sebastián and will lead us down Calle Cristo until we reach the opposite end by "El Parque de las Palomas" (the pidgeons park).

Calle Cristo is a beautiful hilly street paved in cobblestone that crosses the entire city from north to south. According to Puerto Rican historiographer Ricardo Alegría, San Juan's blue/gray pavers are made of iron slag and were brought by the Spaniards in the 19th century to pave the city's streets. They were not brought as ballast as it has commonly been misconstrued by popular belief. During the 20th Century city officials removed the cobblestones from Calle Norzagaray, Calle Fortaleza and Calle San Francisco (the city's main arteries) and rumor has it that they ended up at the bottom of the bay. Others were even more insensitive and paved over them with blacktop.

Today, there is a segment of the citizenry that favors repaving the entire city in its original pavers and closing it off to vehicular traffic. The new pedestrian city would join a select group of European capitals that have adopted this model.

But I wouldn't hold my breath. What has actually happened is that the municipal government has made a lukewarm attempt to pave just a few streets and alleys and has opened them up again to vehicular traffic. You can see the result in a YouTube video that published last year explaining how Puerto Rico's Greatest City Is Being Destroyed. The link is in the reference area.

Walking on cobblestoned streets can be tricky, especially if they are wet. A comfortable walking shoe is your best bet. And if by any chance you're exploring the city on a bicycle, stay away from the wet cobblestones at all cost!

"Seminario Conciliar"

As we start down Calle Cristo we immediately find the Seminario Conciliar, a beautiful colonial building painted in gray with peach trim that you will find on your right hand side about half way down the first block before reaching the intersection with Calle Sol. The building was inaugurated in 1832 as a Seminary College, where many of the Island's priests and secular students trained for over a century. Many of Puerto Rico's finest politicians and thinkers trained at the Seminario Conciliar, including: Alejandro Tapia y Rivera, Román Baldorioty de Castro, José Julián Acosta, Cayetano Coll y Toste and José Celso Barbosa.

Plaza San José to El Parque de las Palomas

Queen Isabella II was instrumental in converting the Seminario Conciliar into the Island's premier educational facility in disciplines such as: physics, chemistry, literature, grammar, rhetoric, arithmetic, geometry, logic, cosmography, metaphysics and foreign languages.

In 1900 the Seminar closed its doors and the abandoned building served as a Catholic school for several years. During the 20th Century the building was returned to its original use for several decades and was finally condemned in 1972.

In 1984 the building was remodeled and for many years it was the home of the Center for Advanced Studies for Puerto Rico and the Caribbean. The building's beautiful architecture and center courtyard were well worth the visit.

Sadly, today it's closed once again. Why. Because it belonged to the Island's Catholic Church, and they declared bankrupsy a couple of years ago.

As we pass the Seminario Conciliar, we continue down Cristo Street and cross the intersection of Calle Cristo and Calle Sol. If you were to make a right at Calle Sol, you would end up once again at Plaza de la Rogativa. If instead, you were to make a left, you would end up at Fort San Cristóbal.

As we continue down Calle Cristo, the next building that you'll find on your right is the famous Hotel El Convento. Inaugurated in 1651 as the Monastery of our Lady Carmen of San José, the building

"El Convento" Hotel

served as a convent for 252 years, until it was closed by the Archbishop of San Juan on December 9, 1903. After this, the building remained vacant for ten years and was sold in 1913 for $151 to the Catholic Church.

During the next 46 years the building went from bad to worse, and served as a department store, a dance hall and even a fleabag hotel, that had no water, electricity or sanitary facilities. In 1957 city officials started looking at El Convento as the ideal site for a badly needed parking structure, and the demolition of the old building seemed almost inevitable.

During that same year, the city of San Juan began an urban renewal program known as Operation Bootstrap, under the guidance of a young and enterprising executive by the name of Ricardo Alegría. In 1959, the building was sold to Robert Frederic Woolworth, heir to the Woolworth fortune for $250,000 to be transformed into a deluxe hotel that was instrumental in propelling business and tourism to the old city.

The Woolworth family spared no expense to transform the dilapidated building into the crown jewel of their hotel empire. On January 27, 1962 El Convento opened its doors and instantly became the most talked about hotel in the Caribbean.

Rather than following the glitzy model of its Condado and Isla Verde counterparts, El Convento followed a more European upscale model, with exquisite dining, posh decorations and luxury in every detail. It's no wonder that it became an instant success among the well to do as the "home of the beautiful people".

But luck was about to run out for El Convento as the Woolworth family decided to get out of the hotel business. In 1971, the hotel was returned as a "gift" to the government of Puerto Rico in lieu of taxes owed.

During the next 24 years the hotel remained in government hands and underwent several administrations with varying levels of success. In 1995 the hotel was sold to a group of San Juan executives, who immediately closed it for renovation.

In January, 1997 the hotel reopened its doors and immediately made the Conde Nast Traveler list of the 25 best hotels in the world. The building is listed as a national historic landmark and is the only hotel in Puerto Rico to belong to the Historic Hotels of America.

Across the street from El Convento Hotel is San Juan Cathedral, the oldest church in Puerto Rico and possibly in the New World. At first glance, the church doesn't look old at all. However, the original structure was built in 1521 under the supervision of Alonso Manso, a Spanish bishop who was the first to arrive in the New World in 1513.

San Juan Minor Basilica

The original building was a thatch-roofed chapel made of wood that fell prey to a vicious hurricane that ravaged the city on October 4, 1526. Reconstruction started that same year and a new stone building was finished in 1529. Once again, in 1615, a hurricane blew away the building's roof, which led to further restoration during the 17th century. In 1917 it was once again restored under bishop William Jones to its present day appearance.

San Juan Cathedral is a rare example of medieval construction in the New World. The remains of Spanish conquistador, and Puerto Rico's first governor, Juan Ponce de León were moved to a marble crypt at the Cathedral in 1908. Ramón Power y Giralt, Puerto Rico's first representative at the Spanish Courts in Cadiz, was returned to the Island on April 6, 2013 and also rests at San Juan Cathedral.

San Juan Minor Basilica

Now, here's something you probably don't know. San Juan Cathedral isn't actually a cathedral. It's actually a Minor Basilica. In 1973, the Roman Catholic Church declared San Juan Cathedral a Minor Basilica, a distinction held by no other church on the Island.

As we walk down the steps of San Juan Cathedral we'll continue down Calle Cristo until we reach "la Capilla del Cristo", a small chapel at the very end of the street. However, there are still a couple of sites worth mentioning before we continue our walk.

Across the street from San Juan Cathedral there's a small tree covered plaza that used to be called "La Plaza de las Monjas". Today it's called "Plaza Felisa Rincón de Gautier" honoring the late mayor of San Juan. The two streets flanking the plaza are Caleta de las Monjas, on your right, which leads to Plaza de la Rogativa and Caleta de San Juan, on your left, which leads to San Juan Gate.

As you start walking towards Capilla del Cristo you will pass a two-story building painted in white, right before the intersection with Calle San Francisco. At the turn of the 20th Century this building was the home of José Celso Barbosa, a black Puerto Rican doctor, sociologist and political leader who graduated Valedictorian of the class of 1880 at the Michigan University School of Medicine. In 1899 he founded the Puerto Rico Republican Party and became known as the father of the statehood movement on the Island. Sadly, his political dreams still haven't come to fruition.

Plaza San José to El Parque de las Palomas

As we continue our walk towards Capilla del Cristo we will arrive at a second intersection, this time with Calle Fortaleza. If you decide to detour towards the Governor's Mansion please remember that you will need reservations to participate in one of the tours. For more details please review chapter three.

By now you'll probable see the small "Capilla del Cristo" sitting at the very end of Calle del Cristo. In colonial times, horse races were held on Calle Cristo starting at the very top of the hill and ending close to Fortaleza Street (there were no "adoquines" back then). Legend has it that a young horseman plunged over the city wall horse and all. As he descended into the precipice he elevated a prayer to a Catholic saint to spare his life.

"Capilla del Cristo" / El Cristo Chapel

As it turns out, the young man lived and the horse died. The Catholic Church built the small chapel to commemorate the event and to avoid similar incidents in the future. The chapel has two large iron gates that are frequently closed. With a little luck you'll catch them open and enjoy the chapel's beautiful gold and silver decorations.

Right next to the Capilla del Cristo there's a small park known as "El Parque de las Palomas" that was closed for some time for renovations and has recently been reopened. The large grey pigeon's that abound in this park are not indigenous to Puerto Rico. The Island's autochthonous pigeon is the "Paloma Sabanera", a smaller tan and brown pigeon that is often seen out in the country. But by the sheer amount of pigeons in Old San Juan, and particularly at this park, it would seem like they've been here forever.

El Parque de las Palomas is an excellent spot to relax, enjoy a cold beverage and take in the excellent view of San Juan Bay.

If you enjoy this book please take a minute and write us a brief review at Amazon. And don't forget to visit Puerto Rico By GPS where you'll find additional information, pictures, audio, videos and GPS maps to every attraction in Old San Juan.

Finally, if you love the beach, don't forget to check out my other book: "Puerto Rico Beach By Beach" where you will find detailed information about Puerto Rico's most wonderful beaches. The link is in the reference section.

El Parque de las Palomas to Plaza Colón

Our eighth chapter starts at the Parque de las Palomas and will lead us across the city to Plaza Colón.

At first glance, this chapter might seem uneventful, as we enter a more commercial area of the city. But, as you'll soon discover,

"Parque de las Palomas" / The Pigeons Park

most of the history in this chapter lives within the very same commercial facades that render it unapparent.

As we leave the "Parque de las Palomas", we'll walk up Calle Cristo and immediately turn right on Calle Fortaleza. This street crosses the city from east to west and extends from the governor's mansion to the Tapia Municipal Theater in front of Plaza Colón. However, Calle Fortaleza is predominantly a commercial street with very little historical or site seeing interest.

As we reach the first corner we'll be standing at Calle Fortaleza and Calle San José. We'll be turning left at this corner, but before we do, there are several points of interest that I thought I might mention. If by any chance you need to mail a postcard, there's a small US Post Office on the next corner with Calle Fortaleza. Also — a couple of buildings further down on the right, on 152 Calle Fortaleza— there's an unassuming white washed building that was the birthplace of Luis Muñoz Marín, Puerto Rico's first elected governor after the 1898 US invasion.

Muñoz Marín was a poet, journalist and politician trained at Georgetown Preparatory School in Washington DC. In 1920 he joined the Puerto Rican Socialist Party headed by Santiago Iglesias Pantín (https://en.wikipedia.org/wiki/Santiago_Iglesias), where he advocated for Puerto Rican Independence from the United States and defended the rights of the Island's workers, who in his view, were being neglected by the political forces of the time.

In 1932 he joined the Puerto Rican Liberal Party headed by Antonio R Barceló and became the editor of the party's official newspaper "La Democracia". One of his famous quotes from this period was: "The press can improve government, but government cannot improve the press". On March 13, 1932 he was nominated as a senator for the Liberal Party and served from 1933 to 1937. In 1937 Muñoz Marin parted ways with Antonio R, Barceló and founded the Popular Democratic Party in 1938.

El Parque de las Palomas to Plaza Colón

He immediately started campaigning in rural areas and was instrumental in eliminating the common practice of paying off rural workers to influence their vote. In 1940, his newly founded party won the senate by a slight victory and Muñoz became the fourth President of the Puerto Rican Senate. In 1944 he won again and served a second term as President of the Puerto Rican Senate. During his years in the senate he helped advance legislation for agricultural reform, economic recovery and industrialization.

In 1947 the US Senate approved legislation allowing Puerto Ricans to elect their own governor. In 1948, the Popular Democratic Party won the election and Luis Muñoz Marín became the first Puerto Rican to be elected governor of the Island in the 20th Century. He governed Puerto Rico for 16 years from 1948 to 1964 and was instrumental in transforming the Island from the poor house of the Caribbean into a full-blown industrial powerhouse.

As you turn left on Calle San José take a look at the peach-colored building at the very corner. At the turn of the 20th Century this was the office of the famous Puerto Rican poet Luis Llorens Torres.

Llorens Torres' parents were well-to-do owners of a coffee plantation in the "Collores" suburb of Juana Díaz, a small town on the southern coast of the Island. He finished high school in the small town of Maricao and moved to Spain to study Law at the University of Barcelona. He then went on to study philosophy and letters at the University of Granada, were he completed his doctorate degree in both disciplines.

His childhood memories of the beautiful Puerto Rican countryside are evident in each and every one of his exquisite poems. The nationalistic nature of his work is known as "criollismo", because of the way it tells the story about the Island's customs and traditions.

Immediately after we turn left on Calle San José we see various important structures. On the left hand sidewalk, right on the corner of Calle San José and Calle San Francisco you'll see a beautiful neoclassical structure built in 1851 on a plot of land that was once the cemetery of the old city.

The building was originally known as the "Real Intendencia" and its functions were similar to our present-day department of the treasury. In 1866 it became a library and a drawing school for secondary education. After that, the building served as the "Diputación Provincial", sort of like a present day Legislative Assembly.

In 1897 the Spanish government granted autonomy to the Island and the building became the new Insular Legislature. After the US invasion in 1898, the building was reassigned to the San Juan Superior Court. In 1984, the building was remodeled and was assigned to its present day function as the Department of State of the Commonwealth of Puerto Rico.

Across the street from the Department of State there's an elegant square known as Plaza de Armas. Its original name was la Plaza Mayor and it was built by the Spanish government at the turn of the 19th century to resemble its much larger counterpart in the city of Madrid.

Plaza de Armas has undergone various modifications during the last two centuries. The original square was paved with a combination of tile from the Canary Islands and black river stone. In 1851, Spanish governor Pezuela added a "salón paseo" or strolling area that was much in vogue at the time in European circles. The new square ended up being several feet above street level and was sarcastically baptized by the "sanjuaneros" as Pezuela's Pantheon.

By the time the US invaded the Island in 1898, the square had once again been brought down to street level, and a small concrete wall with ironwork decorations was built around the perimeter. The Plaza de Armas that we see today was restored in 1992, when the city celebrated the quincentennial of the discovery of America.

El Parque de las Palomas to Plaza Colón

On the northern side of Plaza de Armas we find City Hall, another neoclassical structure built between 1604 and 1789, that resembles Madrid's City Hall in Spain. This building is the only one in San Juan with an archway entrance spanning the entire width of the structure. This is an important detail because colonial law specified that all buildings surrounding mayor plazas had to include archways. Another interesting fact is that Old San Juan is one of the few towns in Puerto Rico in which its cathedral or Catholic Church is not across the square from City Hall.

City Hall has a tourist information center on the first floor and a small gallery with itinerating exhibits. Admission is free.

Our walk will continue east on Calle San Francisco. About a block and a half down from City Hall, on your right hand side of the street, you will see a rather run down building painted tan with white trim that used to be the headquarters of "La Democracia", the official publication of the Puerto Rican Liberal Party of which Luis Muñoz Marín became editor in 1932.

City Hall & "Plaza de Armas"

About another block and a half down Calle San Francisco, on your left hand side, you'll arrive at the Franciscan Chapel, a small church built by the third order of Saint Francis in 1776. The church is part of a larger complex that includes Plaza San Francisco, right in front of the chapel and the old Franciscan Monastery that is presently the Carlos Albizu University.

Right next to San Francisco Chapel and right in front of Carlos Albizu University is a beautiful square called "La Plaza de la

Barandilla". It's the only square in the entire city that is not dedicated to a saint or to a historical figure.

"Plaza de la Barandilla" / "La Barandilla^ Square

As we continue down Calle San Francisco, there is one last point of interest before we reach Plaza Colón. If you look on your right hand side, one door before reaching Plaza Colón you will see an unassuming four-story building painted in gray with white trim that was once the home of "El Buscapié", a liberal oriented newspaper founded by Manuel Fernández Juncos in 1877. El Buscapié was satirical in nature and promoted many socialist ideas such as free education for every child. It quickly became the most popular publication on the Island.

Manuel Fernández Juncos was born in Oviedo, Spain in 1846, but came to Puerto Rico when he was still a small child. He is remembered as one of the Island's most distinguished journalists, poet, author and humanitarian. He was also the writer of the official lyrics to "La Borinqueña", the national anthem of Puerto Rico.

This brings us to Plaza Colón, the beautiful square at the main entrance to the Old City. In colonial times, this square was called Plaza Santiago, because it sat right behind Santiago Gate.

El Parque de las Palomas to Plaza Colón

Imagine yourself for moment in the mid 19th Century. The statue of Christopher Columbus, facing south in the middle of Plaza Colón didn't exist. Instead, there was the statue of Juan Ponce de León that is presently at Plaza San José on Calle San Sebastián. The Government Reception Hall on the left hand side of Christopher Columbus didn't exist either. Instead there was the eastern corridor of the city wall and a substantial part of Fort San Cristóbal that were both demolished in 1897.

This leaves us with the only building of historical importance that we haven't mentioned. The Municipal Theater of San Juan, better known by the "sanjuaneros" as "Teatro Tapia" was built in 1832 and named after the famous Puerto Rican playwright Alejandro Tapia y Rivera. It was designed in the Italian style, as a horseshoe shaped opera house, with three tiers of boxes.

The beautiful neoclassical building is one the oldest freestanding drama stages in the New World and hosts a wide variety of events from ballets, plays, and operettas to modern day theatrical and musical events.

Plaza Colón

If you enjoy this book please take a minute and write us a brief review at Amazon. And don't forget to visit Puerto Rico By GPS where you'll find additional information, pictures, audio, videos and GPS maps to every attraction in Old San Juan.

Fort San Cristóbal

Our ninth chapter starts at Plaza Colón and will lead us up Norzagaray street to the remarkable Fort San Cristóbal.

Norzagaray street is the steep hill that intersects will Calle San Francisco on the northeastern quadrant of Plaza Colón. Fort San Cristóbal has two entrances, one on Ponce de León Ave., which is mostly for cars and tour buses, and one on Norzagaray street, which is mainly for pedestrians. We'll be using the entrance on Norzagaray.

But before we start up the hill, let's take a minute to visualize how large the original Fort San Cristóbal really was. The portion of the fort that you see today is roughly half the size of the original, and it's still the largest Spanish fort in the New World. In 1793, when it was finally completed, Fort San Cristóbal covered over 27 acres and extended all the way down to San Juan Bay. At its highest point, Fort San Cristóbal rises over 150 feet above sea level. Now remember, 18th Century San Juan had no tall buildings and none of the buildings that are presently in front of Fort San Cristóbal existed either. So a sentinel standing at the highest point in the fort could easily see all the way to the edge of the islet towards the east and across the city to Fort San Felipe del Morro towards the west.

In 1897, city officials decided to demolish Santiago Gate, along with a substantial part of Fort San Cristóbal to promote urban development on the eastern side of islet. The demolished portion of the fort included half of the Trinidad Counterguard, the Santiago Ravelin, the Santiago Bastion, and a considerable portion of the dry moat.

Ravelins were triangular shaped forts –also called lunettes– that were built in front of bastions to serve as outer defenses. Later on we'll be looking at "El Abanico", which is the outermost of Fort San Cristóbal's ravelins and was restored by the National Park Service.

Fort San Cristóbal also had a glacis, similar to the barren piece of land in front of Fort San Felipe del Morro that we discussed in chapter number four. This would have been where the Island's Capitol building stands today, along with the old WMCA building, the Casa España, the Athenaeum, the Treasury Department and several other smaller buildings.

After walking up a small portion of Norzagaray Street, we'll be entering Fort San Cristóbal through the western ramp leading to the main gate. Look carefully over the massive wooden doors and you'll see a shell-shaped symbol with an arc over the top. This was the symbol of Saint James, the patron saint of the Spanish army.

Fort San Cristóbal (West Entrrance)

Fort San Cristóbal

As you enter the fort, the first thing on your left will be the ramp leading to the Northern Battery and the guardhouse. In colonial times, the guards at this post would control access to the fort and enforce military discipline. Today, they'll charge you a $10 entrance fee (good for both forts during a 24-hour period) and hand you information about the fort and other nearby attractions. They're also a lot friendlier!

Immediately after the guardhouse you'll see the main square, were Spanish soldiers conducted drills and punished the unruly. But before we walk towards the square, let's take a few steps back and walk up the ramp immediately to the left of the main entrance. Most of the time this ramp is closed to the public, so you'll need to speak with a park ranger for permission. This ramp leads to the North Battery, which was added by the Spaniards in 1897 to defend the north side of the fort from sea attacks. Ordoñez canons at this battery fired the first shots of the Spanish-American War on the morning of May 12th, 1898.

The North Battery also offers an excellent view of the northern side of the city wall, all the way to Fort San Felipe del Morro at the western tip of the islet.

Once we walk back down to the fort entrance we will turn left and enter the main plaza. In colonial times, Spanish soldiers conducted all sorts of military exercises in this square and punished the unruly in ways that today would be considered cruel and unusual. Insubordinate soldiers would be forced to walk between two rows of musketeers who would hit them repeatedly with the butt of their muskets. If the soldier fell before completing his punishment, he would be taken to the infirmary, cured and returned to the square to receive the remainder of his punishment.

At the far end of the main plaza we see the Troop Quarters, a two story building finished in 1733 that had four barrack rooms on each level. One of the rooms has been restored to resemble the typical living conditions of an 18th century soldier. Another holds a scale model of Fort San Cristóbal as it was in 1793.

Make sure to see this model as it will give you a clearer idea of how huge this fort really was. The remainder of the first floor holds the military archive where students and researchers can obtain in-depth information by appointment only. The center stairway leads to the second floor, which in turn leads to a circular staircase that goes up to "El Caballero de San Miguel".

Across the main plaza we find the officers quarters and two round wellheads that sit directly over the fort's massive cisterns. Here you will find several exhibits about the fort's history including replica canons, weapons and life-size figures of Spanish soldiers in uniform.

Like many other things at Fort San Cristóbal, the main plaza serves multiple purposes. It actually sits over five huge cisterns that held up to 716,000 gallons of rainwater, enough to support the fort for an entire year.

The islet of San Juan has no rivers and in colonial times it had no aqueducts either. Spanish engineers worked around this limitation by constructing huge cisterns under the main squares of both forts. Rainwater was collected through channels at each level that lead to the forts cisterns. This also meant that cleanliness was of paramount importance. Animals were not allowed inside the forts under any circumstance.

In fact, modern day Puerto Rico would probably be an English speaking island if the Queen's army hadn't ignored this rule. In 1598, George Clifford, the Earl of Cumberland, attacked San Juan and captured El Morro. However, his fatal mistake was to bring his horses into the fort. Six weeks later, his troops abandoned the city after falling prey to an outbreak of dysentery. Nothing like a little contaminated water to drive the enemy out of town.

On the north side of the square we find a row of vaulted rooms called casemates. The guns in these rooms pointed straight out to sea and their objective was to shoot at the hulls and decks of enemy ships. Their enclosed nature made them practically impervious to enemy fire.

Fort San Cristóbal

"El Caballero de San Miguel" The highest point in the fort!

The last two rooms behind the guardhouse didn't hold guns at all. The last was for the latrines and the one before it was the kitchen.

Right next to the Troops Quarters there's a large ramp that leads to "El Caballero de San Miguel" or cavalier. In military terms, a cavalier is the highest point in a fort or castle, and its purpose is to secure a high observation point from which sentinels can observe enemy operations. In colonial times, a sentinel standing at "el caballero" could see across the entire 47 square mile islet from east to west and north to south. After walking back down the ramp to the main plaza, you'll see three large tunnels on the eastern side of the plaza.

Fort San Cristóbal has an extensive tunnel system that was used to move supplies, personnel and weapons to different areas. The tunnel on your right goes from the exterior ramp to the fort's information area and souvenir shop. The other two are physically underneath the ramp. Of these, the one on the right will take you to the main battery on the second level. Canons on this level protected the fort from both land and sea attacks. However, the number of canons wasn't enough to match the number of embrasures, so they were mounted on wheels and moved around as needed. Larger canons were moved up and down the ramps using a sophisticated rope and pulley system known as block and tackle.

"La Garita del Diablo"
The Devil's Sentry Box
The lowest point in the fort.

If you walk towards the easternmost corner of the second level plaza you will arrive at a lone sentry box that offers an excellent view of several important areas. As you enter the narrow walkway that leads to the sentry box, right before entering the box, take a look down towards your left and you'll see the famous "Garita del Diablo" or Devil's Sentry Box sitting at the very base of Fort San Cristobal.

Spanish soldiers used Sentry boxes to protect the city walls around the clock. Some of these were close between, but others were more distant and solitary. At night the guards would occasionally shout a call to neighboring guards in their boxes so as to check on their whereabouts and keep them from falling asleep.

--Guard, be alert, would shout one.
And the nearest would answer back:
Alert, I am! --

Among all the boxes there was one —the most distant and lonely— that sat close to the water at the very base of Fort San Cristobal. In the silence of the night, the swishing of the sea would produce a noise that seemed as if all the bad spirits were whispering to each other.

Soldiers didn't like this box at all, as rumor had it that strange noises and spirits were heard there through the night.

The night the Devil's Sentry Box got its name it was Sanchez' turn to stand guard. Sanchez was born in Andalusia and was a very fair-skinned lad. In fact, he was rather pale, but was still a very handsome man. His fellow soldiers called him "Flor de Azahar", after the white flower that grows abundantly in the Andalusian region of Spain. He was a member of the Cavalry Regiment, and was also an excellent guitar player.

As always, the occasional cries from one guard to another were heard, but nothing was heard from Sanchez' box. Only the whistling wind and the rushing water of the sea was heard on that pitch-black night. Fear reigned among the other guards during the remainder of the night, not knowing what could've happened to their friend.

At sunrise, they all rushed to Sanchez' box to find out why he hadn't answered.

They found his rifle and his uniform, but Sanchez had vanished without a trace. The superstitious soldiers spread the rumor that he had been surprised and taken away by the Devil. Since that day on, the sentry box has been called "The Devil's Sentry Box".

But very few were aware that Sanchez was in love with a beautiful half-breed girl named Diana. The girl's stepmother didn't approve of their relationship, and Sanchez' commander also prohibited the romance, because of the girl's dark skin.

But Flor de Azahar would play her coded messages on his guitar. At night he would play and sing. In his songs he would communicate with Diana.

One night he sent a message that only she could understand, that said: "Tomorrow at night, go and find your love, because far from your arms, his heart is dying..."

The following night, Diana arose late at night and left her house to find her lover. They met at the Sentry box, where Sanchez was standing guard, and decided to go far away and live together forever.

Diana brought civilian clothes for Sanchez to wear. So he left his rifle and uniform and the couple escaped to the mountains where they lived happily ever after.

As you lift your head away from The Devil's Sentry Box you'll see various other important structures. In the distance you'll see Puerto Rico's Capitol building, which resembles the U.S. Capitol building and sits at the very edge of what used to be Fort San Cristóbal's glacis. As you'll recall from chapter 4, a glacis was a barren plot of land that offered no shelter or cover for attacking forces.

Right in front of the Capitol building you'll see a small triangular fort that sits at the very front of San Cristobal's outer defenses. It's called "El Abanico", because from the top it resembles one of the handheld fans (abanicos) that are so popular among Spanish women.

"El Abanico"

Fort San Cristóbal was a military complex unlike any other that combined layer upon layer of offensive and defensive systems.

Fort San Cristóbal

Would be attackers would find a series of smaller forts called ravelins, which could easily repel less sophisticated forces. Behind the ravelins there was generally a dry moat where attacking forces would become sitting ducks for the forts archers and musketeers. Atop the walls there were bastions, which were equipped with cannons and musketeers and were much taller and harder to overtake. And above it all was "El Caballero de San Miguel", which offered a vantage point covering the entire islet and was also equipped with canons and musketeers.

By any standard, Fort San Cristóbal was a military installation like no other in the New World and the prime example of state-of-the-art military engineering in its time.

This leaves us with only one area of the fort that we haven't discussed. On the northeast corner of the main plaza there is still another tunnel that goes right past the fort's dungeon and ends at the northern end of the dry moat. To the untrained eye, this might seem like an easy way to penetrate the fort. Just go up the tunnel and "voila" you're in the main square. Easy, right?

But a closer look at the inside of the tunnel will prove this kind of plan suicidal. The large grooves that you see every twenty or thirty feet divide the tunnel into sections. If you look close to the floor you'll also see a series of small niches (where there are light bulbs today) that could be filled with explosives to bring down that particular section of the tunnel. By placing large removable doors at the grooves immediately behind each section, the Spaniards could selectively demolish sections of the tunnel and stop attackers before they reached the main plaza.

At the upper end of the tunnel we find the fort's dungeon, a place so miserable that even today it sends chills up your spine. Imagine a place that's hot and humid, constantly dark, where the air was stale and smelled of human excrement. Now throw in some sweaty prisoners, rats, roaches and ticks. Oh yeah, and the only source of ventilation and light is a small port at the end of the room, about the size of a paperback book. This pretty much describes the human living –or dying– conditions inside the 18th century dungeon at Fort San Cristóbal.

"El calabozo" / The Dungeon

On the left wall, as you enter the dungeon, there's a series of drawings made by one of the inmates that is suspected to have been a captain. Experts have come to this conclusion because of the great detail they offer of the ship's sails and rigging. The red pigment used in the drawings is another clue that the prisoner was no ordinary soldier. It's a rare substance that contains a great amount of iron, that when exposed to the salty air would oxidize and become a reddish color. Finally, it would have been close to impossible to make these drawings in the dungeon's pitch-black environment. Therefore, historians suspect that the prisoner had outside help that provided him with some sort of lamp and drawing materials to make his stay less miserable.

As you exit the tunnel, look back over the entrance and observe the little white bomb over the entrance, this will confirm what I was telling you a minute ago about its purpose and design. Im-

Fort San Cristóbal

mediately to your right there's a closed door with two small ports at it's upper left. Place your hand into the ports and feel the cool air coming out. This used to be the fort's powder house and it's the most protected room in the fort. It's designed to keep the powder cool, dry and as protected as possible from enemy fire.

To exit the fort we will go right hand tunnel (of the three on the Main Square and exit through the World War II bunker that leads to Ponce De León Ave. on the south side..

If you enjoy this book please take a minute and write us a brief review at Amazon. And don't forget to visit Puerto Rico By GPS where you'll find additional information, pictures, audio, videos and GPS maps to every attraction in Old San Juan.

Finally, if you love the beach, don't forget to check out my other book: "Puerto Rico Beach By Beach" where you will find detailed information about Puerto Rico's most wonderful beaches. The link is in the reference section.

Fort San Cristóbal to Plaza Dársena

There are two ways to exit Fort San Cristóbal: through the west ramp that leads to Calle Norzagaray and through the World War II bunker that leads to Ponce De León Ave. on the south side. Since we entered through Norzagaray St. let's exit through Ponce de León.

If you look towards the northeastern corner of the main square you will see three tunnels. As you will recall, the one on the left leads to the dungeon and the outer defenses and the one in the middle leads towards the fort's second level. That leaves the tunnel on the right.

Walking down that tunnel will bring you to the World War II bunker where there's a visitor reception area, a souvenir shop, restrooms, the fort's office area and a small theater.

By the way, there's a free audiovisual about the entire San Juan Historic Site that's available in English and Spanish. Ask the guard about exhibition hours.

When you exit on the south side of the World War II bunker you'll be inside one of the fort's many dry moats. Of course, today it's one of the parking areas that leads to Ponce de León Ave.

Just a few steps to the east of the entrance to the parking area you'll reach the intersection of Ponce de León Ave, Norzagaray

Street and Calle San Francisco, where you walked up hill a while ago to reach the western entrance to Fort San Cristóbal.

Government Reception Center

Turn left at this corner and continue straight down the street until you reach a bend in the road right behind the Tapia Theater.

The first building on your left will be the Government Reception Center. Construction started in 1910 and the building opened it's doors in 1913.

This is exactly where the old "Puerta de Santiago" used to stand. "Puerta de Santiago" was the only gate in Old San Juan that connected to land. This earned it the nickname of "la puerta de tierra" or "the gate to land".

But the Government Reception Center has some recent history as well. This is where many of the scenes for Sylveter Stalone's 1989 blockbuster "Assassins" were shot. Remember the bank scene? Well, that was actually Puerto Rico's Government Reception Center.

Fort San Cristóbal to Plaza Dársena

Once you pass the bend behind Tapia Theater you'll find a small square on your right dedicated to Puerto Rican composer and orchestra conductor Arturo Somohano.

There are several excellent restaurants and small bars in this area. It also marks the end of our tour. From here you will have various options. If you arrived on a cruise ship you will see the docks to you left and you will easily find your way back to your ship.

If you arrived by plane, and your taxi dropped you off at Plaza Dársena, you'll be able to catch a taxi right where you stand or you can walk one block west to the corner of Calle Recinto Sur and Calle Tanca, turn left and you'll find Plaza Dársena on your right hand side.

Oh, and just so you know, this corner of Calle Recinto Sur and Calle Tanca was where "La Puerta de España" (the gate to Spain) stood until 1897.

Alejandro Tapia y Rivera Theater

This formally concludes the Old San Juan Walking Tour. If you still have a little more time I encourage you to explore the remainder of the city on your own.

The Old San Juan Walking Tour

Old San Juan is both a bustling city with vibrant life of its own and a living museum where history envelopes you. There are hundreds of great restaurants and bars, wonderful gift shops and dozens of smaller museums and galleries that you can explore at your leisure.

And if by any chance you're staying at one of the boutique hotels in the Old City you'll discover that the city's nightlife is great as well.

If you enjoy this book please take a minute and write us a brief review at Amazon. And don't forget to visit Puerto Rico By GPS where you'll find additional information, pictures, audio, videos and GPS maps to every attraction in Old San Juan. The link is in the reference section.

Finally, if you love the beach, don't forget to check out my other book: "Puerto Rico Beach By Beach" where you will find detailed information about Puerto Rico's most wonderful beaches. The link is in the reference section.

Reference Section

Juan Ponce de León
https://en.wikipedia.org/wiki/Juan_Ponce_de_Le%C3%B3n

Mexican Situado
https://en.wikipedia.org/wiki/Real_Situado

Sir Francis Drake
https://en.wikipedia.org/wiki/Francis_Drake

George Clifford
https://es.wikipedia.org/wiki/George_Clifford_de_Cumberland

Ralph Abercromby
https://en.wikipedia.org/wiki/Ralph_Abercromby

Gonzálo Fernandez de Oviedo
https://es.wikipedia.org/wiki/Gonzalo_Fern%C3%A1ndez_de_Oviedo

Eugenio María de Hostos
https://en.wikipedia.org/wiki/Eugenio_Mar%C3%ADa_de_Hostos

Felisa Rincón de Gautier
https://en.wikipedia.org/wiki/Felisa_Rinc%C3%B3n_de_Gautier

Felisa Rincón de Gautier Museum
http://www.museofelisarincon.com/

Carlos Romero Barceló
https://en.wikipedia.org/wiki/Carlos_Romero_Barcel%C3%B3

José Antonio Corretjer
https://en.wikipedia.org/wiki/Juan_Antonio_Corretjer

Antonio Matos Paoli
https://en.wikipedia.org/wiki/Francisco_Matos_Paoli

Pedro Albizu Campos
https://en.wikipedia.org/wiki/Pedro_Albizu_Campos

Isabel de Trastamara
https://en.wikipedia.org/wiki/Isabella_I_of_Castile

Pablo Casals
https://en.wikipedia.org/wiki/Pablo_Casals

José Campeche
https://en.wikipedia.org/wiki/Jos%C3%A9_Campeche

Alejandro Tapia y Rivera
https://en.wikipedia.org/wiki/Alejandro_Tapia_y_Rivera

Román Baldorioty de Castro
https://en.wikipedia.org/wiki/Rom%C3%A1n_Baldorioty_de_Castro

José Julián Acosta
https://en.wikipedia.org/wiki/Jos%C3%A9_Juli%C3%A1n_Acosta

Calletano Coll y Toste
https://en.wikipedia.org/wiki/Cayetano_Coll_y_Toste

Reference

José Celso Barbosa
https://en.wikipedia.org/wiki/Jos%C3%A9_Celso_Barbosa

Queen Isabella II
https://en.wikipedia.org/wiki/Isabella_II_of_Spain

Ramón Power y Giralt
https://en.wikipedia.org/wiki/Ram%C3%B3n_Power_y_Giralt

Luis Muñoz Marín
https://en.wikipedia.org/wiki/Luis_Mu%C3%B1oz_Mar-%C3%ADn

Antonio R. Barceló
https://en.wikipedia.org/wiki/Antonio_Rafael_Barcel%C3%B3

Luis Llorens Torres
https://en.wikipedia.org/wiki/Luis_Llor%C3%A9ns_Torres

La Democracia
https://en.wikipedia.org/wiki/La_Democracia_(newspaper)

Manuel Fernández Juncos
https://en.wikipedia.org/wiki/Manuel_Fern%C3%A1ndez_Juncos

Teatro Tapia
https://en.wikipedia.org/wiki/Teatro_Tapia

Ordoñez Canons
https://en.wikipedia.org/wiki/Ord%C3%B3%C3%B1ez_guns

Spanish-American War
https://en.wikipedia.org/wiki/Spanish%E2American_War

Arturo Somohano
https://en.wikipedia.org/wiki/Arturo_Somohano

Printed in Great Britain
by Amazon